PUNK NOVEL.

BY BAD AI.

Macmillan Publishing Co., Inc.

New York

Collier Macmillan Publishers

London

Macmillan Publishing Co., Inc.
866 Third Avenue, New York, N.Y. 10022
Collier Macmillan Canada, Ltd.

Library of Congress Cataloging in Publication Data

Bad Al.
    Punk novel.

    I.   Title
PS3550.B3P86   811'.54   79-28429
ISBN 0-02-504630-6

First Printing 1980

Printed in the United States of America

C.K. Williams quote from "Hog Heaven"
in WITH IGNORANCE. Copyright © 1977 by C.K. Williams
Reprinted by permission of Houghton-Mifflin, Co.

William S. Burroughs quote from Introduction to
NAKED LUNCH. Copyright © 1959 by William S. Burroughs.
First Evergreen-Black Cat Edition, 1966.
Reprinted by permission of Grove Press, Inc.

A rabid dog cannot choose but bite.

--William S. Burroughs

I want you to know
that only three people
in the whole fucking publishing business
liked Punk Novel
for any reason whatsoever.
D.D. tried to peddle it but couldn't.
D.C. tried to buy it but she got fired.
Dizzy Miss Lizzie did it.
And nobody--nobody--does it better.
Thanks Big Dick, too,
and Runaround Sue
for making it look like it sounds.

For

The Chocolate Kid

and

The Vanilla Kid

SIDE ONE

HOT STUFF
  (3 MIN 15 SEC)............................
BAND 2
  (10 MIN 47 SEC)...........................
BAD CONNIE
  (3 MIN 1 SEC)............................
HEMORRHOID
  (3 MIN 25 SEC)...........................
WE AIN'T TERRORISTS
  (3 MIN 49 SEC)...........................
A IS FOR
  (3 MIN 50 SEC)...........................
THE FUR IS GONNA FLY TONIGHT
  (4 MIN 10 SEC)...........................

SIDE TWO

MOTHER
  (2 MIN 40 SEC)...........................
YOU THE JURY
  (3 MIN 17 SEC)...........................
GERONIMO AND HOLLYWOOD
  (5 MIN 17 SEC)...........................
HALLOWEEN
  (3 MIN 30 SEC)...........................
HIGH LOW
  (3 MIN 6 SEC)............................
MUTHAH HUBBARD
  (3 MIN 48 SEC)...........................

SIDE ONE

HOT

SO THIS AIN'T A NOVEL
SO WHAT
LOOK HOW YA GROVEL CAUSE YA
THINK IT'S SOMETHIN' HOT.

So this little old lady dies
and the family cries
and pickets won't let
her coffin through the gate,
she gotta wait for
some future date when
the union okays every
last clause and meanwhile
folks just stuff mama
into one of them drawers
and that's because hot damn
ain't the unions just great!

SO THIS AIN'T A NOVEL
SO WHAT
LOOK HOW YA GROVEL CAUSE YA
THINK IT'S SOMETHIN' HOT.

So this em dee shoves up a IUD
and ya don't have no baby,
but yer whole hole is all
twisted up and the metal coil
tears ya up and twenty years
from now ya got a nice big,
healthy, bouncin' baby cancer
and there ain't no answer
'cept ya got what ya paid
for when ya stopped doin'
what ya was made for.

SO THIS AIN'T A NOVEL
SO WHAT
LOOK HOW YA GROVEL CAUSE YA
THINK IT'S SOMETHIN' HOT.

So the United States
Government says majority rules
and yer kid goes to schools
where history's a mystery
and yer tax bucks buy hack books
and the kids are hipper than
the morons they got mouthin' off
at the head of the class,
and how many people ya know
voted for fifth-floor walk-ups
with no heat and nothin'
to eat and who ruled
in favor of all them wars
and twelve-year-old whores
and cars that fall apart
and bars that cut their drinks,
and this big deal majority
fuckin' stinks if they gave us
emphysema and Hiroshima
and Selma and women who grow
up to be Wilma Flintstone.

SO THIS AIN'T A NOVEL
SO WHAT
LOOK HOW YA GROVEL
THINKIN' YA GOT SOMETHIN' HOT.

So yer daddy's
the man of the house
and late at night he
puts on a see-through blouse
and butters his ass and blows
out gas and makes a pass
at somebody else's daddy.
And even if he's straight,
it's always too late or else
he's got an important date
or not now honey it's
the championship game in the
Pac Eight and can't it wait,
and ya rate way down there
after money and an illicit
honey and office politics
and ya grow up too quick
but ya still call him Daddy.

SO THIS AIN'T A NOVEL
SO WHAT
LOOK HOW YA GROVEL
CAUSE YA THINK IT'S SOMETHIN' HOT.

So this is some great work
of art and ya can't tell where
the picture starts or ends
and Friends'll kill ya
in the name of God, and
ya wear what poor people wore
fifty years before and
French faggots call it mod,
and an expensive antique
is a chair with a busted seat,
and restaurants inject
their meat with ox blood
so the world looks juicier to ya,
so ya can lay around in gravy.

SO THIS AIN'T A NOVEL
SO WHAT
LOOK AT YA DROOL AND GROVEL
CAUSE YA THINK IT'S SOMETHIN' HOT.

14

So this is the Department
of Welfare and they don't care
that ya been out of work for
a year with a ruptured spine
and some greasy spic
hooked on wine steals when
he works and makes his boss
look like a jerk and
keeps rakin' in twenty-six
weeks of checks and who's
lookin' out for yer welfare?
Who cares about yer
funny walk and achin' bones
and foot-long scar?
And that spic takes
yer money and spills it
all over a down-neck bar.

SO THIS AIN'T A NOVEL
SO WHAT
LOOK HOW YA GROVEL CAUSE
YA THINK YA GOT SOMETHIN' HOT.

So this is the man who promises
to love, honor, and cherish
the ground where ya stand,
and ya spend forty years
makin' garbage and
stuffin' it into a can
and he rapes ya legal and
puts up a ten-pound
Segal lock to protect ya
when he's not around.
So yer smarter and kinder
and better than he'll ever be,
he's the one with the key,
and then when yer belly's
all out of shape and yer
teeth are gone and yer hands
are chapped down to the bone
and he can leave ya alone 'cause
nobody would look at ya twice,
yer kids put ya on ice and
shove ya into a drawer and
everybody hopes the union
accepts a contract before ya
thaw and everybody still
thinks the unions are nice.
But union's another word
for vice and liberation's
another word for prison,
and only a fool believes
the majority really rules,

and everybody begs to be
ripped off and lied to,
and ain't these tricks slick?
and ain't ya doin' just
what ya oughta, never
muddyin' up the water, spendin'
a quarter of yer money
and time on America Sublime,
America Sublime, on Mickey Mouse
and grease and grime and
undetected unsuspected crime.

SO THIS AIN'T A NOVEL
SO WHAT
LOOK AT THE WAY YA GROVEL
CAUSE YA GOT SOMETHIN' THAT'S
WHAT IT'S NOT,
CAUSE YA GOT SOMETHIN' HOT.
THANKS A LOT.

BAND

Teach goes and busts his leg all up
skiing down a country
the day before school starts, and we get
his physics lessons on closed circuit.
"Count your blessins,"
the head of the department tells us,
and we're lucky they could work it
so class don't close,
and stick out your nose is everybody here?
I don't hear nobody cheer. Do you?
Bleach Job chases the mob of us out back
and continues to crack her knuckles
and we're out the door and she keeps talkin'.
That's what we moved to the suburbs for,
"So you and your friends
could have a nice big yard to play in";
and as she was sayin' how
ten of us would destroy her
seventy-five-thousand-dollar house,
Louie Louie calls her a louse,
and Ramona gets even with her mom
by openin' her blouse
and givin' us a squeeze and a tease,
and the ten of us gang-walk downtown
and make scared little ladies
step all the way 'round
to the other side of the street.
Preach sits us down one by one
and cites Christ
and begs us to give him the zip gun
and begs us to zip up our mouths

when he's in the middle of a sermon,
and Lennie is playin'
with vermin in his pocket,
and Deadbeat cops a locket
off Mrs. Preach's dresser,
and Hesh says that proves that
although his collar's turned around,
his sex life ain't.
Man, what a drag this week has been
and it's only the beginning,
like the first inning of a game
that don't mean nothin' in the standings.
We're all standin' in line and
there's four features at the Bijou;
did you see the one about
how crime don't pay and the one where
love means never having to say, "Sorry,
you have to keep your feet off the seat,"
and the one where everybody lives
and nobody gives a damn?

                    LET'S BE A BAND
                    BE A BAND
                    BE A BAND
                    MAKE A STAND
                    TAKE A STAND
                    LAND A BAND
                    SUCK A SONG
                    FUCK A SONG
                    WHAM BAM RAM
                    WHAM BAM RAM.

We got Louie Louie on the wall;
he bangs his head against the wall
and gets out all the grass
and the tests he can't pass
and his mother's ass,
which all of our fathers have grabbed and stabbed
at one time or another.
Bang it, Louie, there's nothin' else to do-ee,
make yer brains into chop suey,
make the blood run black and gooey.

                    LET'S BE A BAND
                    BE A BAND
                    BE A BAND
                    MAKE A STAND
                    TAKE A STAND
                    LAND A BAND
                    SUCK A SONG
                    FUCK A SONG
                    WHAM BAM RAM
                    WHAM BAM RAM.

We got Ramona who strips to the waist
and gives everyone a taste
and then cups one hand in the other armpit
and pumps out farts that sound like loose shit
and pumps out her broken cherry
from her night up on Mulberry
when a big black junkie
raped a seven-year-old honkie
and Ramona's mother never pressed charges
cause she didn't want the neighbors
to hate her or bait her sexy little girl.
Pump it, Ramona, it's a gas, it's a blitz,
it's a Blatz, it's a Pabst, pump that pit
till the house can smell the shit.

       LET'S BE A BAND
       BE A BAND
       BE A BAND
       MAKE A STAND
       TAKE A STAND
       LAND A BAND
       SUCK A SONG
       FUCK A SONG
       WHAM BAM RAM
       WHAM BAM RAM.

We got Jungle Jim on his own red meat;
he spreads his feet and starts to beat.
He's hittin' his thin skin
and his big blue vein
and maybe now he won't go insane
'cause girls won't touch him;
he took his sister to the movies
one Saturday night
and she let him
practice his moves at the front door,
and when he tried to kiss her
she let him and started to pet him,
and he said, "Don't you care
I got pimples and sometimes I'm simple,
and I got bad breath and the touch of death?"
and Sis held it while he took a piss,
and it was still big as a bat
and that's why the girls are afraid,
they've never been laid by a dick like yours,
even whores would lick their lips
and roll their eyes
thinkin' of sittin' on somethin' that size;
and she put it in her mouth a while
and let it trickle down her throat
and Jungle Jim spread out his coat,
and they call that incest where I come from.

Jungle Jim, ya can't come in;
ya did it to yer sister, she told me;
if I do it to you, Mama's gonna scold me;
yer outta yer mind, Jungle Jim;
yer gonna go blind, Jungle Jim;
stick it up yer own behind, Jungle Jim.
Hell, we'll give ya a spot out front
where ya can do yer stunt;
we'll throw a red light on that red meat,
and they'll clap when ya beat.
Go, Jungle, whack it, jack it.
Go, go, Jungle,
give the little ladies a great big treat.

                    LET'S BE A BAND
                    BE A BAND
                    BE A BAND
                    MAKE A STAND
                    TAKE A STAND
                    LAND A BAND
                    SUCK A SONG
                    FUCK A SONG
                    WHAM BAM RAM
                    WHAM BAM RAM.

We got Iggy on the throttle,
he sits on his bike drinkin' a bottle
of anything hard and guns the engine
and it sounds like a jackhammer,
and once it got him thrown in the slammer
'cause he tore up the steps of a motel
right into the office and hit the bell
and took a swig
and started to yell for service.
Gimme a room, gimme a quart,
gimme a T-bone, gimme towels,
gimme a French maid, gimme, gimme, gimme.
And the clerk knew a cop named Jimmy,
and the judge gave Iggy a room
and a towel and that was all.
Race her, Iggy, let her rip,
blow yer broken hip right outta the pipe.
Blow away the sideswipe and that big hypodermic
and the pain and sufferin' loot ya got
and how hot Harley was
and that nice buzz ya picked up downstairs
at Daddy's bar in the boom boom room.
Ya need zoom zoom room;
ya need speed, Iggy, speed is what ya need,

ya gotta fly, ya gotta be high,
ya gotta wheel and weave and leave
those fat cat friends of yer parents
and those jerks at school
and those jerks at work
and those jerks
at the Marine Recruiting Office
and all the jerks with their penny ante perqs
chokin' in yer exhaust. No matter what it costs.
Go, Iggy, rev it up, Iggy,
whip them horses, Iggy,
ya ain't goin' nowhere,
but yer gettin' there fast.

                    LET'S BE A BAND
                    BE A BAND
                    BE A BAND
                    MAKE A STAND
                    TAKE A STAND
                    LAND A BAND
                    SUCK A SONG
                    FUCK A SONG
                    WHAM BAM RAM
                    WHAM BAM RAM.

We got Jo Jo on his thumbs,
he twiddles 'em 'cause he's numb.
He can't feel anymore,
he's been through it all before,
a wife, a kid, he had a ball,
and then it rolled under a car
and down a sewer,
and it's all over for Jo Jo,
who used to walk down the street
whistlin' "Teenage Marriage."
They were both eighteen,
she was prom queen,
and they couldn't live without each other
one more minute.
Jo Jo's mother-in-law-to-be played
"O promise Me" on a spinet,
and it all started right there
in his wife Bev's living room,
and it ended there too with gloom hangin'
in the air where they strung crepe paper
and flowers the year before.
Now Jo Jo paces the floor.
Bev shot heroin behind her knee,
which was like smokin' behind the barn,
so no one would see,
and the last piece of paper
with her name on it said OD,
and the baby had to go cold turkey
and didn't make it,
and Bev's mother had to fake it
when she said, "God knows what He's doing."

Twiddle, Jo Jo, spin them thumbs
till they turn up for luck,
till that foot-and-a-half coffin
gets buried in yer memory,
and pretty young things don't smell like Bev
and walk like Bev and talk like Bev
and find a vein and make it bulge
and indulge themselves behind yer back.
Hey, there's gonna be clappin'
and shoutin', will ya hear it?
Hey, there's gonna be a light show
every night, Jo Jo, will ya see it?
Oh, Jo Jo's gonna be all right.
He may be numb, but he sure ain't dumb.
Come on and twiddle that thumb,
twaddle that thumb.

> LET'S BE A BAND
> BE A BAND
> BE A BAND
> MAKE A STAND
> TAKE A STAND
> LAND A BAND
> SUCK A SONG
> FUCK A SONG
> WHAM BAM RAM
> WHAM BAM RAM.

We got Hesh on comb,
he combs his hair and he streaks it too,
and last week he was takin' a leak
and he took a peek at the guy
standin' at the next block of ice
and how nice it was
and how gay it is to be out of the closet
after all these years.
Comb, Hesh, comb it all out,
the never knowing for sure
till one pure piece,
he said he's been to Nice,
tried to lure ya into
his "rooms" he called it
and the two of ya balled, it
was cool ass,
it was so tight,
but it was so right.
Comb out the perfumed soaps
ya hid under yer socks
and yer unexplainable interest
in antique clocks
and also little musical figurines,
so delicate, so dainty,
such intricate machines.

Comb, Hesh, with a graceful arm
and debutante charm
and yer funny little strut
like an old school marm.
Give 'em a little Jagger,
throw 'em a little dagger,
do yer mincin' swagger, comb!
Comb out the knots and tangles
and dead bed bugs.
Tease 'em, Hesh.
Blow dry 'em, Hesh.
Give it to 'em nice and easy,
give it to 'em short and sassy,
give it to 'em up the assy.

LET'S BE A BAND
BE A BAND
BE A BAND
MAKE A STAND
TAKE A STAND
LAND A BAND
SUCK A SONG
FUCK A SONG
WHAM BAM RAM
WHAM BAM RAM.

We got Thorazine Zeke on headphones,
his own headphones blaring into his head,
and at regular intervals
he lets the audience hear
by pullin' a phone away from his ear
and the music is so loud the crowd moans
and the crystal chandeliers rattle and break
and it's like an earthquake
with people runnin' all over each other
and screamin' and the shatterin' glass
and the crackin' walls, and then
he lets the phone snap back to his ear,
and all ya can hear is Zeke
tappin' his foot while the yappin'
keeps zappin' his Thorazine brain.
Do it again, Zeke.
How do ya stand it, Zeke?
They got ya so dazed,
yer brain's like a sponge,
yer eyes are half crazed.
But ya got the beat behind yer eyes
and ya got the rhythm in the back of yer head
and ya can take music
that would wake up the dead.
Snap it, Zeke,
make us all weak in the knees,
how can ya stand it?
Well, ya been doin' it for twenty years,

electricity shootin' through yer ears,
tee vee, radio, stereo, tape recorders,
cartridges, eight tracks, CB,
anything ya can plug into yer mind
and leave the world behind
goes in one ear and stays in there,
turns gray in there,
'cause the loudness is all that matters,
no matter what it shatters.
And one time yer old lady pulled the plug
and ya wound up in the bug house
listening to the Thorazine make ya dream.
We won't do it to ya, Zeke,
we'll keep that shock therapy
goin' full blast
'cause yer part of the cast.

> LET'S BE A BAND
> BE A BAND
> BE A BAND
> MAKE A STAND
> TAKE A STAND
> LAND A BAND
> SUCK A SONG
> FUCK A SONG
> WHAM BAM RAM
> WHAM BAM RAM.

We got Lennie who gets
his sounds out of his pets.
He squeezes his parakeet
and it squawks and flaps against
the wire cage and feeds Lennie's rage,
and he steps on his cat's tail
and ya can hear it wail in the last row;
that Lennie really puts on a show.
If ya ask him why, he'll cry
and poke out his doggie's eye,
and between his grunts and karate yells
and cursin' ya can hear the gory story
how his parents broke his bones
and yelled shut up when he groaned
and locked him in his room
and beat him with a broom handle,
fed him dung and stung him with a hat pin,
hid him in the attic in the dark
and left him in the park overnight
at age six.

Let it go, Lennie, spit it out, burn
that little lamb till we hear it bleat,
hold that fish up in the air
till it crackles in the heat
and we flip-flop in our seats
and ya cut off Bossie's teats
and ya smother birdie's tweet
and we're all screamin' to yer beat.

> LET'S BE A BAND
> BE A BAND
> BE A BAND
> MAKE A STAND
> TAKE A STAND
> LAND A BAND
> SUCK A SONG
> FUCK A SONG
> WHAM BAM RAM
> WHAM BAM RAM.

We got Deadbeat, too,
who rattles like death
and holds his breath
and his face turns gray
and the audience always turns away 'cause
they can't stand to see a young man die.
But they won't give him a job
or give him a stake
or let him make his own way,
and life don't pay when yer dead broke
unless ya stand on a stage
and pretend to choke
like a ninety-year-old about to croak.
Deadbeat's been on the skids
for a solid year
since he graduated high school
and it feels like a lifetime.
Yer hungrier when there's so much food around,
sleepier when the world sleeps so sound,
and Deadbeat's gotta prowl all night
to pick up a buck here a buck there
and keep from real crime
that'll get him the chair;
just a stick-up or a pick-up

to pay the rent;
just a bank job or a blow job
and a government check.
Rattle, Deadbeat, gasp
and grasp yer last, wheeze
and snort and totter at the brink
of Potter's Field,
grow a gray stubble
and take out yer teeth,
take out yer teeth,
put on yer wreath,
put on yer wreath.

                    LET'S BE A BAND
                    BE A BAND
                    BE A BAND
                    MAKE A STAND
                    TAKE A STAND
                    LAND A BAND
                    SUCK A SONG
                    FUCK A SONG
                    WHAM BAM RAM
                    WHAM BAM RAM.

And we got me, Bad Al,
bangin' his hand with his fist
'cause he missed the boat
and there's a moat around everything good
and everything that stinks
is on his side, my side.
I got doctors
that sew ya up wrong on my side;
I got singers
that forget the words to the song;
I got teachers high on coke
and cancer makes ya smoke,
and when's the last time ya heard
a really funny joke?
I got appliances up the ass
and a shortage of gas and oil
and nobody plays according to Hoyle.
I got kids with scrambled brains
and Pepsi Cola in mah veins,
and every time it rains
veterans with metal pins gulp aspirins,
and, oh, if only they didn't volunteer,
if only that shit green moat wasn't here.
I got cars that kill and cops that kill
and chemicals that kill and
frozen swill in schoolhouse cafeterias.
I got girls that will
and carry the pill and don't give ya a bill,
but they make ya pay the rest of yer life
and it's worse than a wife,
and everybody under thirty is dirty,
and everybody over thirty is sick,
take yer pick, do it quick,
the moat's gettin' bigger now.
Ya know what it's like to be a nigger now.
Lookin' in. Ya know what it's like
to be thin and mean
and nobody talks to ya
and nobody cares what ya think
and ya figure ya stink
the way they turn up their nose,

but they pull down their hose 'cause it's in.
Hit it, Bad Al.
I got crossword puzzles
and the time and need to guzzle booze
and nothin' to lose and nothin' to gain
and tee vee keeps flashin' in mah brain
and I can't turn it off
and I got this dry cough
just from walkin' down the street.
But, man, I got mah beat.
Ya can't get that away from me.
Make me wear yer clothes
and go to yer schools and learn yer rules
and eat yer food and drive yer cars
and get drunk at yer bars,
but ya can't take away the fact
that I'm pissed, and ya can't
con me into openin' mah fist.
No, ya can't stop me,
ya can't stop any of us,
ya can't break up our band.
That's all there is.
In this whole crummy life. Our band.

> LET'S BE A BAND
> BE A BAND
> BE A BAND
> MAKE A STAND
> TAKE A STAND
> LAND A BAND
> SUCK A SONG
> FUCK A SONG
> WHAM BAM RAM
> WHAM BAM RAM
> WHAM BAM RAM
> WHAM BAM RAM
> WHAM BAM RAM
> WHAM BAM RAM
> BE A BAND
> BE A BAND
> BE A BAND
> BE A BAND

There's six or seven of these guys
that Connie sits for, and
any minute they're gonna explode
if they don't shoot their lode
'cause my Connie, she does some
bad bad numbers.
Mr. Jones don't make any bones,
he hates his wife and hates his life,
and they're always goin' out to dinner.
But he wants to be a sinner,   ·
grab Connie one night and
squeeze her and please her,
and she wears a tight sweater
when she sits for Mr. Jones
and no bra and there are shadows
where her nips stick up, and
they make that Jones sausage sizzle.
"Have a nice dinner;
don't worry about anything,"
and she brushes by his arm and
the hairs on the back of his neck

go dancin', and I'll bet Jonesy
can't keep his food down
thinkin' 'bout Jonesy Junior
prancin' around with Connie and her tits.
And he knows Bad Al is gonna show,
and we're gonna do it in his bed,
and his Missus has to drag him out,
he never wants to go,
and Connie watches him

WALK OUT THE DOOR
BALLS SCRAPIN' THE FLOOR
SINGIN' BABYSITTER FANTASY
JUMP INTO MAH PANTS WITH ME
JUMP INTO MAH PANTS WITH ME
JUMP INTO MAH PANTS WITH ME.

Mr. Smith has a daughter,
and he bought her jeans like Connie's,
and she had to lose five pounds
before she could pull 'em on and
pull her dad's with Connie charm.
Oh, what a perfect ass
each time his baby walks past,
and it wiggles and sways and
Smitty pays mah devil woman
two bucks an hour so he can study
the real thing and then bring home
jeans and diet books till

baby looks like his dream.
He sits there in the dark movie
watchin' twenty-foot fatales
slide across the screen
and dares to put his hand between
mah Connie's Spaulding cheeks, and
he pops another goober goober goober
and makes a fist and
twists it in up to his wrist,
and Mrs. Smith is a one-way woman,
if you know what I mean,
and Smitty's crazy scheme
is gonna make him bleed if he
don't go insane first or try
to fuck his own daughter in the ass
or make a pass at a policewoman.
And Connie, she's so bad,
I love her when she's bad,
she paints on them jeans and
sashays around Mister Smith's
living room and "Isn't it cute"
comes from that fifty-year-old
beaut he calls honeybunch.
And Smitty knows damn well
I'm gonna grab that swell
of fresh flesh he can taste and
wrap it 'round mah Bad Al face,
and Connie always makes sure
to drop somethin' and bend down
and pick it up just as Smith
is ready to leave so she can
give him a good show, and while
she's down there, she watches him

WALK OUT THE DOOR
BALLS SCRAPIN' THE FLOOR
SINGIN' BABYSITTER FANTASY
JUMP INTO MAH PANTS WITH ME
JUMP INTO MAH PANTS WITH ME
JUMP INTO MAH PANTS WITH ME.

Mr. White is very cool;
he don't let us see him drool,
but we go through his bedroom
drawers and laugh at his Spanish
postcards and his special creams,
and what a ream he must give
the White lady with this,
holdin' up a mighty fine vibrator
with little plastic bumps,
and it's the ugliest pink thing,
and Connie says the string is
so you can pull it out of a pussy
swallow before her happy holler
brings down the whole fuckin' town.
And then there are those photos
I guess he uses instead of No Doz,
big wonderful healthy cocks
with little girls stuck on the ends,
suckin';
it even sends a shiver through Connie,
and she says "That's what he wants,
my tiny little teeth and my soft
pink tongue and my fuzzy wet lips,"
and Whitey sips his gimlet

through a straw and pictures
Connie's jaw
opening just a crack
and swimmin toward his cock,
and her lips are like a soft
rubber fitting, and Mrs. White
is sittin' there with bridgework
and root canal scars and
can't stand hubby's imported cigars,
and that bad girl of mine never
fails to flash her pretty teeth
and run her tongue along her lips
and whistle and blot and plot
and watch him

WALK OUT THE DOOR
BALLS SCRAPIN' THE FLOOR
SINGIN' BABYSITTER FANTASY
JUMP INTO MAH PANTS WITH ME
JUMP INTO MAH PANTS WITH ME
JUMP INTO MAH PANTS WITH ME
JUMP INTO MAH PANTS WITH ME
JUMP INTO MAH PANTS WITH ME.

HEMOR

RHOID

Mom goes to this shrink,
and Sis goes, too, and they're tryin'
to get along with each other,
but every time they put three feet
in the same room I can hear
the hissin' and spittin' all the way
down in the cellar where I'm sittin'
with a million amps of rock,
beatin' my cock, wantin' to sock
those two outta mah life.
So this shrink, Gunther's his name,
he's got eyeglasses thick as
shot glasses and an even thicker accent,
and he don't charge Mom a cent 'cause
this is a community service; Gunther,
he wants to implicate someone else.
Crazy Mom and crazy Sis ain't enough.
Gunther does his stuff by blamin' me,
too. There ain't no Dad,
and ain't it sad, but brother Bad,
that boy should come in and see me.
'Cept this punk don't wanna be shrunk.

MAYBE YOU CAN SHRINK A HEMORRHOID
BUT MAH HEAD'S A WHOLE OTHER THING.

So I go take a look one day,
and what does he say; he says
"Let's talk about your relationship
with the other members of your family."
And I'm gonna go along for the ride
'cause this shrink's leavin' himself
wide open for the kind of fun I love.
I'll get him.
I know how to get him good.

MAYBE YOU CAN SHRINK A HEMORRHOID
BUT MAH HEAD'S A WHOLE OTHER THING.

So we do this and that and piss away
an hour a day with bullshit chitchat
'bout how I'm scared to say what I feel
and examples using an onion peel,
and why don't I look at it
from their points of view,
and what is a mother to do,
and baby Sis looks up to you,
and I know just what I'm gonna do.

MAYBE YOU CAN SHRINK A HEMORRHOID
BUT MAH HEAD'S A WHOLE OTHER THING.

I'm settin' him up now,
feedin' him textbook tidbits
like I got the hots for Sister,
and once I spiked Mom's tea
with Listerine, and Shady and me
like to try different things,
ya know, with our bodies, ya know,
when no one's lookin', ya know,
and he has a real big one,
and boys will be boys, ya know,
and I keep findin' things in mah room
but I don't know how they got there:
books and records and bottles of perfume
and five-and-ten-cent trash,
and the amazin' thing is,
I never have any cash,
so where does all this stuff come from?
Do ya suppose they're presents?
And Gunther resents how wrapped up
his case seems to be.
Oh yeah, and I throw in a little
pyromania for good measure.
Mah symptoms are this big bleak
treasure and all he has to do is dig
a couple of inches down and shovel

the psychological crap around.
And I goad him and I pull him in,
and once in a while
I kick him in the shin just so
it don't seem too easy, and our chats
are gettin' less and less breezy,
and old Gunther's gettin' anxious,
and I see he's got this tic
I never noticed before,
and when he takes off his glasses
he's blind as a bat,
and one day it was freezin'
and he forgot his hat
and he talked about that for forty minutes.
Gunther's at the deep end;
Gunther's at his wit's end;
Gunther's at the deep deep end of his rope.
And he's a dope.
And I give him hope.
And that's the joke. Get it?
He wants me to take
a battery of shrink tests
just to see where I come out.
At first I play it coy
and tell him I'm too nervous,
and I toy with the old man.
"It's just for my records,"
he assures me, and now I got him
where I want him for sure,
and I give in,
and here goes his battery of tests
with pictures and questions
and draw mah mom and draw mah pop
and what does this plop of ink
look like to me? What do I see?
Cannibals eatin' a butterfly,
six old ladies about to die,
the king of kings asleep in a sty,

a boy with a snake hangin' out of his fly,
and I draw mah Mom
so she barely fits on the page,
and mah rage makes the pencil point break,
and then for Pop a casual dot,
and that's it,
and I swear he took a shit
right then and there sittin'
in his high-back chair.
So. Now the results are in
and according to the conclusions
I should not be allowed out.
I should be under lock and key
and therapy, and Gunther is just
about to break the news to me
when I stand up and say,
"So long; I'm all through.
I don't want to talk to you."
"Please, please, don't go away,"
he stands and begs and it's
the first time I ever saw him stand up,
and I throw him this real mean sneer
like I do and tell him again positively
I'm through.

MAYBE YOU CAN SHRINK A HEMORRHOID
BUT MAH HEAD'S A WHOLE OTHER THING, GUNTHER.

Bad Al, I know you did it just for fun,
but these are your results,
no other one, only you, Bad Al,
the great pretender.

UH-ONLY ME, THE GREAT PRETENDER, UH-O...

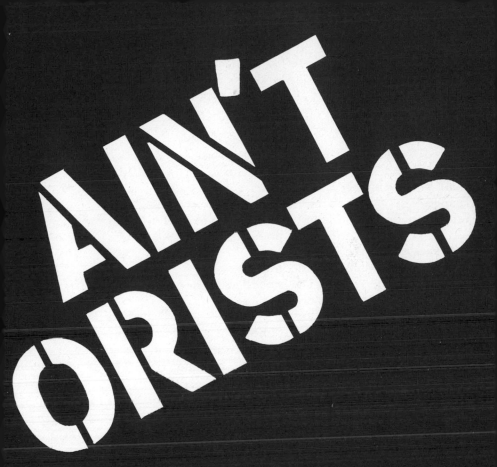

WE AIN'T TERRORISTS, WE JUST LIKE TO
BLOW UP BUILDINGS
'CAUSE WE HATE BUILDINGS
WE HATE EVERY BUILDING ON THE BLOCK
SO WE TIE TNT TO A TICK TOCK CLOCK.

Bad Al, he hates office buildings
'cause his sister worked in an office building,
and well-dressed men
rubbed up against her in the elevator
and her boss loosened his tie one night
and said she could get ahead
if she gave him head
right there under the desk
all scrunched into the kneehole, see?
And when he wasn't doing that,
Sis says, he's always going down
to the department of alcohol,
cigarettes, and guns in Washington
and defending the use of open blouses
and penthouses in liquor ads.
And Bad Al works in an office building
too and makes a little less money
than he needs each month,
but he knows he ain't ever gonna quit
unless somebody blows it
right out of the ground.
Right out of the sky.

BAD AL AIN'T A TERRORIST   HE JUST LIKES TO
BLOW UP BUILDINGS
'CAUSE HE HATES OFFICE BUILDINGS
HE REALLY HATES OFFICE BUILDINGS
HE HATES EVERY OFFICE BUILDING ON THE BLOCK
SO HE TIES TNT TO A TICK TOCK CLOCK.

Mean Moe, he hates the unemployment office
'cause he has to go there every two weeks
and rub cheeks with the scum of the earth
to collect what he's not worth.
When he was young
he wanted to be a fireman,
and he still did
when it came time to be something,
and he saved a baby's life one night
and put out false alarms
more than anything else
because his territory was full of bums
who thought it was real funny to bust the glass
and make the men tear ass down the pole.
But then they fired him,
which he thought was
a particularly funny thing to do to a fireman;
the city couldn't afford his squad
and packed it in,
and wrestlin' a hose and savin' babies
was not in demand,
and it didn't mean anything
when he looked for another job.
But he got one slingin' hash,
and then the back alley trash caught fire,
and the luncheonette burnt to the ground
and Mean Moe had to look around
for another place to go.
So meanwhile Mean grabs his unemployment
and can't stand standin' next to
this jerk who's always there
and never did a heroic thing in his life.
Or his wife who comes to collect, too,
and all the niggers and all the spics
and all the women who're turnin' tricks
and still pickin' up free checks.

MEAN AIN'T A TERRORIST, HE JUST LIKES
TO BLOW UP BUILDINGS
'CAUSE HE HATES UNEMPLOYMENT OFFICES
HE REALLY HATES UNEMPLOYMENT OFFICES
HE HATES EVERY UNEMPLOYMENT OFFICE ON THE BLOCK
SO HE TIES TNT TO A TICK TOCK CLOCK.

Dirty Gerty, she hates cheap hotels
and nasty swells who sometimes tie her up
and beat her up and knock her up
and pay and go away,
and sometimes she wishes she could
see 'em again and cook 'em dinner
and darn their socks and one of 'em
could tickle her wen with his tongue
and make her feel young again.
She's very pretty
and has an easy time finding marks,
and the men are always surprised
by how cool she is,
but she's burnin' up inside
because she's got her pride,
and, besides, there's nothin' else to do
even though she doesn't need the money anymore
'cause she bought everything she wanted,
and she puts it in the bank
to thank her future children
for not goin' to sleep in cheap hotels.
But just to make sure,
she better get rid of those fallin' down dumps
where two friends jumped
and the man at the desk is always fat
and once a rat scared a john out of his skin.

DIRTY AIN'T A TERRORIST, SHE JUST LIKES
TO BLOW UP BUILDINGS
'CAUSE SHE HATES CHEAP HOTELS
SHE REALLY HATES CHEAP HOTELS
SHE HATES EVERY CHEAP HOTEL ON THE BLOCK
SO SHE TIES TNT TO A TICK TOCK CLOCK.

Shades walks in and he's had it with school
up to here, putting his hand over his head.
He'd rather be dead than teach those kids
the same shit he had to swallow,
but there he is havin' to follow
the same school plan from A to Z,
and he doesn't wonder why the boys
look out the window and he doesn't wonder
why the girls look at the boys.
This afternoon he tried to smuggle
sci fi into their minds,
but word got out, and there were
flying saucers in the teachers' lunchroom.
How dare you corrupt the plan, one man screamed.
The penmanship teacher broke her nib
and the physics fuddy spilled primal soup
down his bib, and who do you think you are
and what's the matter with you
and don't you value your tenure and,
good God, those kids aren't even seniors!
Shades takes off his shades,
and his eyes are sad,
and this is the first time we realize
just how bad he feels.
He peels a city check off his roll
and takes a stroll while
we decide whether we want to go that far.
But later we're all crazy at some bar
and go, Shades, go; blow, Shades, blow,
blow 'em all to kingdom come 'cause
when they graduate, they're all dumb anyway,
and we understand, we understand.

WE AIN'T TERRORISTS, WE JUST LIKE TO
BLOW UP BUILDINGS
'CAUSE WE HATE SCHOOLS
WE REALLY HATE SCHOOLS
WE HATE EVERY SCHOOL ON THE BLOCK
SO WE TIE TNT TO A TICK TOCK CLOCK.
TICK TOCK. TICK TOCK. TICK TOCK.

59

A IS FOR

Sheena's nephew, he's two,
is here from the midwest
while Mama and Papa take a rest in Acapulco.
We all want to help Sheena out
and take care of little Joe,
teach him everything we know,
give him the get-up-and-go he needs back there
where they don't even comb their hair
till bedtime.

A IS FOR THE MAN WHO SELLS MONKEYS
    ON A STRING.
B IS FOR LADY HIPPO'S BIG LONG THING.
Z IS FOR ZOO WHICH IS HOME FOR ME AND
    YOU.

So we strap him on the back of mah bike
and hit the turnpike,
and we black up his lungs wheelin' through
the tunnel feelin' very fast and hot
'cause look what we got, a two-year-old
who ain't ever been told what's what.
Now this here's the zoo, Joey;
this here's where you go when
ya don't want animals to tear ya apart
and chew on yer heart.
This one's a spider, Sheena tells him,
pointing to the giraffe.
It lives on apple cider
and eats two-and-a-half times its own weight
every quarter hour.

A IS FOR THE MAN WHO SELLS MONKEYS
   ON A STRING.
B IS FOR LADY HIPPO'S BIG LONG THING.
Z IS FOR ZOO WHICH IS HOME FOR ME AND
   YOU.

That's the king of the jungle;
listen to that ferocious gobble;
watch him wobble in his pen;
that red skin danglin' from his chin
is called a mane; once ya meet a lion,
ya ain't ever the same;
don't he make ya feel small;
don't he make ya want to crawl away?
And this is a frog, see his long trunk;
and the one with the hump is a skunk,
and the one standin' next to Sheena
is a laughin' hyena.
He's got twenty monkeys on a string,
and he laughs at everything everybody says
as long as everybody pays.
The scar on his head
is where they made him half-dead;
the glass in his eye's the wrong size;
he sold the gold in his teeth
for the monkey stand, and there's
sand beneath his feet in his dreams.

A IS FOR THE MAN WHO SELLS MONKEYS
   ON A STRING.
B IS FOR LADY HIPPO'S BIG LONG THING.
Z IS FOR ZOO WHICH IS HOME FOR ME AND
   YOU.

So then we take him to lunch at McDonald's,
and when his Big Mac comes,
we call it Beef Wellington,
and his shake is a nice Dom Perignon on ice,
and we're throwin' down the pommes frites
by the handful when suddenly
little Joey says he has to go poo poo.
Poo poo? Man, this kid don't know shit.
Joey needs a lesson in anatomy,
how ya pee and shit
and come on home with me;
Sheena and the boys
will show ya the real thing.

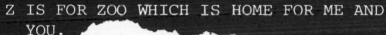

HEY, A IS FOR THE MAN WHO SELLS MONKEYS
   ON A STRING.
B IS FOR LADY HIPPO'S BIG LONG THING.
Z IS FOR ZOO WHICH IS HOME FOR ME AND
   YOU.

This mother here, Joe, gets big
when ya rub it, and Smellbad
decides to dub it a cockadoodledoo,
and the stuff that comes out ain't poo poo,
it's a mother lode, it's love à la mode,
it's what ya rode a thousand miles to hear.
And when it's clear, it's piss, Joey,
and it smells like this, Joey,
and Sheena sticks
his yellow Pamper in his face,
and it's a good thing to do
on the whole human race, Joey.
Now if Sheena will kindly do the undressin',
it's time for a lesson in female fixtures,
which is just a mixture of cockadoodledoo
and a few folds and flaps and bags,
and her tits are so big they sag,
and Joey seems to recognize something.
These are boobs, Joe, dumb ass boobs,
stupid rubes, pumped up outer tubes,
and ya kiss 'em and ya miss 'em
when yer upstairs in yer room
early in the mornin' makin' love to yer sheet
and the heat makes cockadoodle grow.
Want to have a baby?
Just stick a boob in yer ear.
And this fuzzy thing down here
is where the doctor takes a smear
to find out if you're hot to trot;
boys like it a lot; it gets 'em hot;
it's called a knish, and it's ticklish,
and the young boy is foolish
who don't take a peek in there
even though he gets a mouthful of hair.

Go ahead, Joey, touch it,
hold on to the handle and take a gander,
take a goose, squeeze out some juice.
Want to be a rich, famous, powerful,
important citizen of this land?
Always have a hot knish in yer hand.

HEY, A IS FOR THE MAN WHO SELLS MONKEYS
    ON A STRING.
B IS FOR LADY HIPPO'S BIG LONG THING.
Z IS FOR ZOO WHICH IS HOME FOR ME AND
    YOU.

Well, we're all feelin' pretty good 'bout
the education of little Joey
'cept for just a few more pieces of information:
like murder is good and ya can eat wood
and stop means move yer legs real fast
and cuttin' off balls is a real blast
and the stuff in your nose is worth money
and late at night it always gets sunny
and when yer mommy and daddy ain't comin' back
they say they're goin' to Acapulco
and if ya get a lobotomy
ya gotta wear a yarmulka
and fire feels real nice in yer hand
and always suck off a rock 'n' roll band
and always soil yer Sunday clothes
and the only real things are UFOs and

A IS FOR THE MAN WHO SELLS MONKEYS
    ON A STRING.
B IS FOR LADY HIPPO'S BIG LONG THING.
Z IS FOR ZOO WHICH IS HOME, WHICH IS HOME,
    WHICH IS HOME FOR ME AND YOU.

THE
FUR
IS
GONNA
FLY
TONIGHT

Ya know what we need?
Ya know what we really need?
We need to turn to the person next to us
and punch 'em right in the face.
We need one big knockdown, no-holds-barred,
rock-'em sock-'em, free-for-all brawl.
Like I was tellin' somebody the other day,
"Hey, it's easy to get through life
without a scratch,
without a mark,
without a scar,
without a little inside-out flap of skin
to tell folks who you are."
Can ya dig it, man?
Everybody haulin' off at the same damn time?

YOW! OW!

So I'm sittin' here
and I'm not doin' anything,
watchin' the tube, ya know, and I volunteer.
I'm willin' to strike the first blow.
C'mere, Jungle Jim; I call him over,
and he saunters to where
I'm groovin' goony eyes and ga ga on the Gong Show
and I don't look like I'm about to let go.

YOW! OW!

Oh boy, did that feel good.
I knew it would.
I smash Jungle Jim smack in the puss,
and I cut mah fist on his buck teeth,
and both his eyes start to close,
and the blackest blood I ever seen
spurts right outta his nose,
and I say, "Pass it on, Jungle."
Well, that starts it all right.
Before this fat black bitch
with a high thin voice
gets five notes into her song, bong, gong,
the whole room's jumpin' like the film broke.
I mean everybody's hittin' everybody else;
Five Feet of Heaven in a Ponytail's   0
got her teeth locked around
California Dreamer's ankle
and Pillar of Society's
got one knee on Middle America's neck
and Senior Citizen is just swingin' wild;
he punches the wall and it gives in
and won't fight back,
and when his fist connects,
it sorta goes bloop bloop;

the press is here to get the scoop,
and the Marines have landed to clear the poop,
and, alley oop, Teen Angel gets herself
shot-put right through the window,
and, oh boy, this is what I been waitin' for.
now the fight is in the streets,
now we'll see some fur fly.
Yeah, and broken heads and busted chops
and split lips and dislocated hips
and splinterin' shins
and purple eyes and strangled necks
and chomped-up ears and lots of tears,
you coulda drowned in all them tears,
and moanin' and wailin' somethin' awful
and gaspin' and chokin' and gaggin'
and I ain't braggin' but
ya know who started it all?
Bad Al got the ball rollin'
and bones grindin' and flesh rippin'
and the fur is really flyin' tonight.
I just sort of sit back and take it all in.
I just sit back and watch
ya take it on the chin.

YOW!   OW!

Let me put it to ya this way:
I'm somewheres between eighteen and thirty-five
and I can't make the kind of bread
I'm supposed to want
and all the girls are so damn easy
and all the guys are so damn pussy-whipped,
and mater's too busy havin' a nervous breakdown
and pater's too busy
takin' his weddin' ring off in the morning
and puttin' it back on at night,
and my alcoholic senator
ain't never done nothin' right,
and ya can't stand around
shootin' baskets day and night
so why not fight? You tell me.
Is there a better way to get it all out?
"We'll see," says Officer Joe
as he grabs me like I'm a cat
and escorts me into his patrol car
without even opening the door,
and a couple of good whacks

with old billy'll make me all silly,
and they gotta gimme a nudge
when it's my shot with the judge.
So I walk up to his bench very serious
and I'm still a little delirious,
but I'm cool enough to make a fist
and throw it like a Koufax fastball
smash into judge's mouth.
And naturally they give me back the same,
twistin' my arm, wrestlin' me to the floor,
crackin' a few ribs, ya know,
and pretty soon the whole room is crazy,
and don't they see they give me what I want
and I give them what they want?
But no, they don't,
and next thing ya know I'm in a cell
and my black leather jacket's gone
and my black pants and my black turtleneck
and my black and white sneaks,
and the guy in the bunk over mine speaks.
"Whatcha in for?"

AND POW!
OW!

I give him the same,
bashin' his brains against the iron bars,
givin' myself a few fresh scars,
and there they come again,
the bullyboy guards,
puttin' out their lit cigars on my face.
So this time they throw me in solitary,
ain't no one there and nothin' to do,
no tee vee, no fag pussy, no nothin',
and I don't feel any different
than I did before when I caught
ol' Jungle Jim a good one.
Well, that's the answer,
no question about it.
Got to swing out and hit.
Got to level life and sweep it into a stink pit.
Got to drive yer wheels over a pedestrian's heels.
Got to stick yer knife into somebody's life.
Me, I'm no dummy. I been to school.
I read and write and stay up late at night
watchin' art movies in mah gray bedroom,
and mushrooms grow under the covers,
and I got a lover who's the same as me;
one time she looks up from lickin' mah balls
and says is this all there is?
Well, then, let's fight,
and she throws a right,
and the lights, the lights they go on.
Not off. On.
So I'm an advanced human being, see,
I can deal with solitary
'cause I know the way out.
And I reach out mah arm
and I swings that arm 'round and around,
and I get it whippin' pretty good,
and ya look in
and ya think it's a blur and then

POW! OW!

I hit myself right in the middle of mah face,
I hit myself right in the middle
of the whole human race,
and I go flyin' across the cell into the wall,
and all the air gets whammed outta mah heart
and throat and head,
and someone else might think I'm dead,
but, uh uh, I was dead before.
Now I'm sprawled out on the floor.
Alive.
I really knock myself out.
I really do knock myself out.

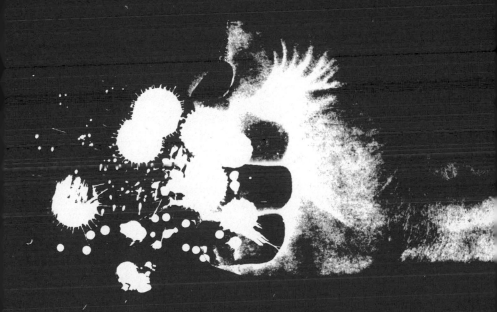

SIDE
TWO

MOT

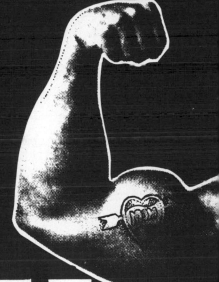

HER

My mother gets dizzy.
She stands up to answer the phone
and starts swaying like she did
when her friend Sid
played sax in the Catskills
during the big band days.

I GOTTA TAKE MAH MOTHER APART
PUT HER BACK TOGETHER AGAIN.

No physical cause, her doctor said,
it's all in her head,
but there's nothing there.
Al, honey, what do I do?
I can feel my hand squeezing
my part of the phone real hard.
Well, don't do nothin',
stop doin' nothin', never do nothin',
ya get nothin' from nothin',
ya stink when yer nothin',
ya die when yer nothin',
ya cry when yer nothin',
ya sigh when yer nothin'.

I GOTTA TAKE MAH MOTHER APART
PUT HER BACK TOGETHER AGAIN
FEET FIRST
STICKIN' UP OUT OF THE HEARSE
BRAINS LAST
I GOTTA MOVE FAST
MAH MOTHER'S FUTURE'S BEEN HER PAST.

So she lets go,
and I hear this far off banging
that tells me she fell,
and I yell like a foreigner away from home.
The hell with lunch.
I gotta take mah mother apart.
My car starts up half-way there,
don't fail me.
The tires wobble on the macadam,
don't fail me.
I gotta take I gotta take I gotta take
mah mother apart.
I gotta break I gotta break I gotta break
the goddamn door off the hinges,
rushing in like Superman
and picking up the broken wing of a mother
fluttering and muttering my name,
and I do it all with one hand.
I prop her up
and her head tilts heavy over to one side,
and I think the fall did it,
and the dizziness made her fall,
and the tee vee made her dizzy.
So I kick the screen in,
and a panelist bites my toe
and won't let go and keeps screamin'
outta the corners of her mouth
that she's willing to go all the way.
All the way. Yay. Mommy, you're tired.
Your friends are dyin' one by one,
and you can't stand the white
in the hospitals.
White nights won't let you sleep.

I have a good idea, let's reminisce.
Remember when you were Lucy
and you stuck your hand into a mailbox
to get back that mis-sent letter
and couldn't get it out
and the cop came and you made
that funny face and that funny noise
and inside the mailbox was a man
from the FBI taking yer prints?
Remember when you were Margaret
and father came home
and told you he was canned
and not to worry 'cause he knows best
and you said "Where can you get another job
that pays so well,
and what the hell do you do, anyway?"
Remember when you were proud
to be Mrs. John Walton
and you baked a birthday cake
for the littlest daughter
out of a diseased chicken
that stopped laying eggs
and you stuck a lit twig in its craw
and the stench made everyone laugh
when baby Elizabeth blew out her candle?
I prop her up
in front of the smashed tee vee set
and call up her friends
who hurry over and sit with her
and tell her she's not the only one.

Minnie's got a bad hip
and a dead drunk she has to forget.
Nell's got cancer up and down,
and she went to a party
in someone else's gown
'cause she's lost another nine pounds.
Listen to them, Mother.
Betty knits.
Gertie reads Harold Robbins.
Flossie plays canasta.
Each one of 'em got something to do.
I can tie my own shoe.
I eat sweets when I want.
I smoke dope and whack off with soap.
But in an hour or a little less,
these elderly ladies
only keep track of the hours now,
they are quiet.
One drops off, dead, Nell,
a funny color on her head, a funny smell;
another one, another one.
I gotta take mah mother apart.
She has her own little recovery group,
but the members can't be reached.
Her husband's dead.
Her friends are dead.
The phone is dead.

FEET FIRST
STICKIN' UP OUT OF THE HEARSE
BRAINS LAST
I GOTTA MOVE FAST.

YOU
THE
JURY

What a jerk I was, barely fuzz on my face
and I musta been spaced
when I poked mah nose into Dem and Rep rows.
I swear all the time I was there
I was pullin' for the truth.
Even when I pulled open
the curtain in that redressin' booth
I was certain I was rightin' wrongs.
But now I'm writin' songs because I'm pissed,
'cause a fist still runs the show,
'cause no matter who I voted for
he would have missed,
'cause all I got was my name
on a mother-fuckin' jury duty list.

JURY DUTY

JURY DUTY

JURY DUTY

JURY DUTY

JURY DUTY

SAY IT FIVE TIMES REAL FAST,

IT'S A MIND-TWISTER.

JURY DUTY

YOU THE JURY

JUSTICE IS A REAL BLAST,

BROTHER AND SISTER.

THE WHOLE WORLD STANDS ACCUSED.

THE WHOLE WORLD STANDS ABUSED.

BUT ME, I BEEN EXCUSED.

Me and The Knife they called him
before they hauled him in,
me and Rutherford Brown
was how they introduced him as they accused him
of buryin' two inches of ice-cold steel
into the commonweal,
me and him,
me and Rutherford The Knife Brown
made eye contact,
made a sort of pact,
signed a sort of soul contract.
It was him against me
and the outraged citizenry
of the outraged community
of the whole not-to-be-out-outraged
country 'tis of thee,
and I guess the ambulance chaser
for the state caught it,
'cause when my number came up
he was ready to audit
everything I said in my defense.
"No, I don't know the defendant,
the lawyer, or the witness,
and I never sat on a case like this,
and I never was the victim of a crime.
Yes, I'm sure I can be fair."
Please excuse juror
number two-two-one from the chair.

JURY DUTY

JURY DUTY

JURY DUTY

JURY DUTY

JURY DUTY

SAY IT FIVE TIMES REAL FAST,

IT'S A MIND-TWISTER.

JURY DUTY

YOU THE JURY

JUSTICE IS A REAL BLAST,

BROTHER AND SISTER.

THE WHOLE WORLD STANDS ACCUSED.

THE WHOLE WORLD STANDS ABUSED.

BUT ME, I BEEN EXCUSED.

Officer M. Angel,
Badge three-eight-oh, Beat seven,
is tryin' to get to heaven
heavin' heavies into jail.
Got a dope pusher and a subway masher
and a bank-job stasher
and a sick, sad flasher
and I see this M. Angel in the washroom
groomin' his slicked-back hair for
when he gets up in the witness chair
to seal the case
and deal himself an ace
and steal the years from the jury's peers.
But number two-two-one was too fearless,
and when I was done I was peerless.
"No, I don't know the defendant,
the lawyer, or the witness,
and I never sat on a case like this,
and I never was the victim of a crime."
"He's lyin'! We know each other!"
Fuckin' guardian M. Angel stands up
and shoots his gun hand at me
and shouts his slander at me
and I take a gander at the judge
whose expression don't budge
and I nudge
the prospective juror next to me
so he can see my prospective victory.
"Your honor, that cop is full of shit.
I'm sure I can be fair."
Please excuse juror
number two-two-one from the chair.

JURY DUTY

JURY DUTY

JURY DUTY

JURY DUTY

JURY DUTY

SAY IT FIVE TIMES REAL FAST,

IT'S A MIND-TWISTER.

JURY DUTY

YOU THE JURY

JUSTICE IS A REAL BLAST,

BROTHER AND SISTER.

THE WHOLE WORLD STANDS ACCUSED.

THE WHOLE WORLD STANDS ABUSED.

BUT ME, I BEEN EXCUSED.

The plumber got on a murder case,
the short-order cook got arson,
the retired postman
was the foreman for a rape,
and some poor sucker
who couldn't escape watched a trucker,
a clerk, a soda jerk, a butcher,
a secretary, a nurse to a veterinary,
a man who rebuilds transmissions,
a beautician, an electrician,
a waitress, a projectionist,
and a housewife toss his lousy life away.
Everyone got on a case but me.
Maybe it was mah height,
maybe it was mah weight,
maybe it was because
the first morning I got there late
(I had a fuckin' date)
or maybe mah hair
or the kind of clothes I wear
or the way I slouch down in mah chair
and look like I don't care.
Maybe they think
I'd disregard the prosecution
and disregard the defense
and only pay attention
to mah own evidence.
Well, yes. Hell, yes.
I would set 'em all free
so they can go back on the outside
and be as bad as me.
Please excuse juror
number two-two-one from

JURY DUTY

JURY DUTY

JURY DUTY

JURY DUTY

JURY DUTY

GERONIMO

AND HOLLYWOOD

This time when my cuz
chuckled and ribbed me
and hinted 'bout all mah chicks,
I fixed him, fixed him good,
fixed him up with Hollywood,
that's what she calls
the pictures of herself.
He says, "Are you kiddin' me?"
and seems afraid I'm not,
and there's a little bubble of snot
that shows how he's breathin'
thinkin' about a night on the town
with a beautiful New York City model
that owes me a favor.
In and out it goes. In and out.

YA KNOW, I THOUGHT I WAS BEIN' KIND
BUT I BLEW HIS OTHER MIND
NO NO, I WAS BEIN' KIND
NOW NOW HE'S INTO HIS BEHIND . . . IT'S
THE TIMES.

So I get on the phone,
and Hollywood's home
and this is it,
a date with my cousin,
he's all right, he'll treat ya right.
"Some favor," she says,
and I wonder if she's Connie
who went out with everybody in high school
or Ellen who had puffy cheeks
and Rick told me she gave him a job
in study period once,
but I didn't believe him,
and I don't believe the worst
about Rita the cheerleader either

when I imagine the football team
kickin' her around
under the grandstands.
Hooray for Hollywood...
ya know, I was bein' kind.
Ya know, he was about to change his mind.
But this was too good to pass up or mess up,
and I stayed with him
the whole time he was getting dressed up,
and Canoe, I suggested,
but he detested the fancy smells
and wore his sailor bells
and lizard belt and unbuttoned his shirt
so his curly blond hair flashed
and caught the light just right
if he stood a certain way
in the bathroom under the flat,
flattering fluorescent tube.
I was bein' kind.
I was tryin' to make him shine
after all these years of feelin' bad
that I knew models
and who did he meet
in the Alibi Lounge and Don Juan's
and the Major Winfield Hotel and Hiway Haven?
Some he told me about,
like a widow with three kids
and she drank too much
and a Spanish waitress
who refused his tips and his hips
but smiled a big golden smile
and sucked a sugar cube
and wouldn't let him take her out
because her husband was a maniac
and Tricia (the pisher, he called her)
who liked spending his money

and dumped him when the truth came out
that he wasn't a hot shot,
not by a long shot,
he had this Good Humor wagon
and he couldn't make it go.
I thought I was bein' kind.
But I couldn't stay with him all night.
So I took one last look
and said he was cool,
go get her, go get her,
get in under her sweater,
slip five under her sweater,
I told him go get her,
ain't nothin' like bare tit,
and he wants to know
what kind of girl is she?
Would she like to go to a show
or just dinner,
and he's counting his tens,
and I tell him hens lay
no matter what you pay.
This is Dreamsville for cousin Hesh;
he keeps checking her address
every five minutes along the Turnpike
trying to guess if Fifty-third Street
runs east or west
and what's the best way to her door.
All he can think about
is how he looks between his legs
as he enters the tunnel,
and I'm across the river
and certain things occur to me now
about Hesh and me growing up together.
In the green locker rooms of our youth
he always turned his back to me
slippin' in and out of his

basketball shorts or tennis shorts
or gym shorts or hockey shorts.
And he didn't go to his 3A picnic
or his Hop or his Prom,
and we never ran into each other
at Jo Ray's, a pink hunk of tail
curling around his arm.
Bullethead and Bee Bee
and Red and Yussie
and Crazy Gerry Geronimo Giambelli and Hesh
were thick as thieves,
and they played ball in the streets
and in the playgrounds
and on the stoops and in empty lots,
and Yussie was older and always had a car,
and they all still keep in touch pretty much.
Bullethead jumped ship
and sued the Navy for fuckin' him up
and collects monthly compensation
while his whole life is a vacation
and he's been in jail for this and that.
Yussie runs a nasty installment route
and talks about never wearing a jacket
that's got a hood on the first of the month,
'cause those niggers'll hide in the hallways
and grab ya by yer hood
and stick a shiv cross yer neck
and cop all yer welfare check cashin' money
and laugh like it's funny
when ya gulp and fart and wet yer pants.
Bee Bee's dead
and Red got married for a year
and then his wife and kid took a walk,
and Red laid in bed for a long time
before they found him and brought him home,
and nobody likes hangin' out with him anymore

'cause he's so depressin',
and he runs errands for a delicatessen uptown,
and he's especially friendly
to the kids that come in
'cept he calls 'em all Wendy,
which is his daughter's name, I think.
And Geronimo ran off the brink,
he could run faster than anyone
and was crazy, too, like the time
he took a bike down Summit Avenue hill
and it had no brakes
and the only way to stop
before Summit met a busy intersection
was to crash into a parked car
and sort of pop up free
and roll over the hood
and not even come up with a scratch;
Geronimo missed both wars
'cause he was too young and too old,
and it killed him
so he did stunts on a motorcycle
and appointed himself
a one-man vigilante band
and took care of his neighborhood,
and when the cops found out
he joined the force and shot a speeder
that he chased for ten miles
and finally caught up with
and they suspended him,
and Hesh thinks Geronimo kills cops now,
like the one who got it
on Broom Street two weeks ago.
I'm figurin' he must be there by now
as I'm half-watchin' the tube
and glommin' chips and Hesh rings her bell.
He feels like a swell

and confidence is brimming in him now
as Hollywood lets him in.
She's the best thing he's ever seen
with her Swedish-blond hair
and movie boobs and tight jeans,
and Hesh knows the smell of grass
and can't keep his eyes off her ass
all the way up three flights.

I WAS BEIN' KIND
BUT I BLEW HIS OTHER MIND.

And Hollywood tells him she got hung up
and sorry she's not ready,
it'll just take a minute,
and drag on this a while, handsome,
while she starts to unbutton her silk blouse.
Hesh is searchin'
for someplace else to look,
but there's not a painting
or a book or a magazine or a pet
or a plant or a window with a view
or anything else to do,
and he doesn't even realize
that he's buttoning his shirt up
while Hollywood is buttoning hers down.
So he takes a drag and sits real cool
and she's got no underpants
under those jeans,
and I was bein' kind
but it blew his other mind.
When they were kids, they daydreamed
about Mickey Spillane chicks
doing their tricks,
and Hollywood is standin' there
just about naked and asks Hesh

to help her off with her boots,
stickin' her leg up on his lap,
and he's starin' right at it,
ya know, but no no,
and he gulps and farts and wets his pants
with the wrong stuff,
and maybe Crazy Gerry ain't so tough,
and next time I see him,
he's got this big powder puff
and he doesn't turn his back to me this time
because he doesn't care who knows.
Hesh is philosophizin' there on the Sitz bath,
and I'm combin' my hair,
and he dries his ass
and beats powder on with his big puff
and offers me stuff
that'll blow my mind.
Another time.

I WAS TRYIN' TO BE KIND
NO NO, I WAS BEIN' KIND
NOW NOW HE'S INTO HIS BEHIND . . . IT'S
THE TIMES.

Go go, powder yer buns, Geronimo.
Go go, powder yer buns, Geronimo!

HALLO

WEEN

We're all sittin' around
one night not knowing what to do
and suddenly we're puttin'
double-edge razor blades
into Halloween apples.
"We can be heroes"
is screeching outta the speakers,
and Lizzie is so intent
she drools on all the apples,
and Fat John is eating every other apple
and mining every other apple,
and me, I'm thinkin'
a stinkin' trick on us would be
to put a half dozen of these killers
in a basket full of regular apples.

IT'S RUSSIAN ROULETTE, MY PET
TWENTY TOES AGAINST THE TEE VEE SET
AH PUFFS ON MAH CIGARETTE
AND STEADY CRYIN'S WHAT WE GET.

That's what I sang to myself
the night the rubber broke,
and holy smoke
here we are hiding blades in a fruit
that looks like the inside of a lady
when you cut it open.
It's Fat John's idea
'cause his kid's so fat and she smells
and boys don't want to touch her.

So she stays up in her room
rubbin' Al Pacino against her blubber,
and the flow of fifties sad songs
got warped in her head somehow,
and even though the words don't make sense
and even though she don't know the words
the tunes slither in her limbs
like a poison snake,
and Fat John has to take himself
away from dinner and chug upstairs.
"What's wrong, Cinderella?"
He calls her that, the brat,
"Good girl, good girl."
He tells her that, the brat,
'cause she cleaned her plate up there
in her room where she hides all afternoon
and won't even come down suppertime.
"Holy Good God Shit!"
What is it? What is it?
It smells like pus. It stinks like us.
It's in the closet.
It's in the shoe bag.
Pork chops, lamb chops,
veal patties, salmon croquettes,
apple pie, liver and onions,
weeks of treats she was s'posed to eat.

IT'S RUSSIAN ROULETTE, MY PET
TWENTY TOES IN SILHOUETTE
AGAINST THE BLINKING TEE VEE SET
AH PUFFS ON MAH CIGARETTE
AND STEADY CRYIN'S WHAT WE GET.

It was Lizzie's idea
'cause her kid wets the bed
and plays with the head
of his dick till it's red,
and she's afraid he'll rape someone
and she'll be called by the police
and have to fill out a long report
about how difficult it's been
raising a boy without a father
and how she took him to the zoo
to watch the baboons and lions,
and once she asked a guy she was seeing
if he'd let her kid watch him peeing.
Oh, she didn't know what to do.
The books didn't say what to do.
The pills don't do what they should anymore
in that hospital they put him in.
Ten rooms on the floor,
his is farthest from the door,
and he sticks things into his body.
They found him hangin'
on the doorknob by his ass,
his eyes like glass.
He jammed a pencil in his eye;
the little girl in the next room
started to cry, and she's still cryin',
and her mother and father
blame it on Lizzie's boy,
and, see, he raped someone
after all is the point.

IT'S RUSSIAN ROULETTE, MY PET
TWENTY TOES IN SILHOUETTE
AGAINST THE PIN DOT TEE VEE SET
AH PUFFS MAH CIGARETTE
STEADY CRYIN'S WHAT WE GET.

It's my idea, I guess,
'cause I got a kid, too,
and he's not quite right.
He stutters and jumps
and his mind's a blank.
He's got me to thank.
He ought to yank that cigarette
outta my mouth, ya know.
Do ya understand?
So we're goofin' and smokin'
and nothin's funny, but we're laughin'
anyway, and the doorbell rings
and I open up the door
and Fat John and Lizzie
are crowding around.
"Trick or treat."
This ain't no trick, I know that.
Otherwise, I'd just bash her with mah bat.
Come in, little girl,
pick an apple out of the basket.
She's a bum. Daddy's shirt and hat
and baggy old pants and cork smeared
on her little girl cheeks,
and we're the ones look like geeks
when it's Halloween.
'Cept it isn't Halloween.
It's Monday or three o'clock or spring.
It's everyday for Fat John and Lizzie
and Crazy Al, and the little bum girl
is going to get her treat.
She picks a bright apple
and bites into it right away,
and we all turn our heads
and one of us yawns.
It's Russian Roulette, my pet.
Her father is a Viet vet.

He pushes open the door
and wants to know
what's going on in there all this time.
He's just in time to see her
tear her lip and tongue
on the razor blade that was inside
the bright apple she picked out.
"Who's the one?" he demands.
He grabs Lizzie by her hands
and shakes her till she tells him me,
Bad Al, me, I'm the one he's looking for.
I give him a sneer and say,
"Hey, there's always
one bad apple in the bunch."
He throws a punch.

IT'S RUSSIAN ROULETTE, MY PET
TWENTY TOES IN SILHOUETTE
AGAINST THE SLEEPIN' TEE VEE SET
AH SUCKS MAH LIP, AH SUCKS MAH TEETH,
AH SUCKS MAH LIP, AH SUCKS MAH TEETH,
AH SUCKS MAH LIP, AH SUCKS MAH TEETH,
AH TASTES THE LUMP, AH HEARS THE THUMP,
AH DUMPS THE CHOW, AH SHOWS HER KID HOW,
AH BRAINS MAH OWN AND PUFFS AND PUFFS
MAH CIGARETTE
STEADY CRYIN'S WHAT WE GET.

"Treat," we all holler.

LOW

OH MAN, WHAT A POKER GAME WE HAD
IT WAS BAD
IT WAS SAD
WE BET EVERYTHING WE HAD
AND BIG DICK CALLED "TIME" AND ONE
OF US SAID "HAH, TIME IS ALL I GOT
LEFT."

So Big Dick was checkin' the table,
then he gives his cards a check,
then he stares at the unused deck,
and he rubs his neck,
and he doesn't know
whether to go or throw 'em in.
There's a lot at stake:
Simple Simon, the stockbroker,
he starts to shake
when he thinks about life
without the lot of it
he's thrown into the pot,
his Porsche watch for openers,
his inscribed silver flask on the second hit,
pocket calculator,
and now fourteen-karat dog shit
on a Cartier chain; it's insane.
But he raises with his seat on the exchange.

IT WAS BAD
WE BET EVERYTHING WE HAD
AND BIG DICK CALLED "TIME" AND ONE
OF US SAID, "HAH, TIME IS ALL I GOT
LEFT."

Rotgut was boozy-eyed
and his girl pried 'em open wide,
and he kept forgettin' where he was
and shoutin', "I object, Judge,"
and shufflin' through imaginary briefs.
Gucci attache lay open on the table,
and it was stuffed with
under-the-table cash
lawyers don't have to report,
and because he was a sport
he called Simple Simon's bet with his pet,
a hyperactive little Yorkie no one wanted
'cause it kept scattering the pot
into their laps,
and Bad Al said, "I think it's got to pee."

OH MAN, IT WAS BAD
WE BET EVERYTHING WE HAD
AND BIG DICK CALLED "TIME" AND ONE OF
US SAID, "HAH, TIME IS ALL I GOT
LEFT."

Doc Badbee, he was there,
his walkie-talkie where-are-you-I-need-you
beeper under his chair;
Doc pushed five hundred Quaaludes
into the game
and disposable syringes and a
solid-gold plate that told his name,
and he had this cool-ass poker-face habit
of peekin' at his cards through
a big silver circle over one eye,
and when it was his turn to buy,
he reached into his jacket pocket
and came up with a handful
of every color capsule
the boys had ever seen,
and Bad Al tried the one
that looked like a jelly bean,
and for ten seconds all his cards
looked like queens.

YA SHOULDA BEEN THERE, IT WAS SO BAD
WE BET EVERYTHING WE HAD
AND BIG DICK CALLED "TIME" AND ONE
OF US SAID, "HAH, TIME IS ALL I GOT LEFT."

We were there in Big Dick's house,
and he had nothing but bets
everywhere you looked.
He threw in his Persian rug
and his stereo
and paintings right off the wall
that he had done himself
and one by some guy we never heard of,
a Nikon and a microwave,
and he gave the table all the loot
he picked up from this or that shoot
in some high-falutin' penthouse
where all the hot props
were on the house
and in went the models' dresses
and their modacrylic tresses
and yer guess is as good as mine
where ya draw the fuckin' line.

OH, MY, BUT IT WAS BAD
WE WAS BETTIN' EVERYTHING WE HAD
AND BIG DICK CALLED "TIME" AND ONE
OF US SAID, "HAH, TIME IS ALL I GOT
LEFT."

Me, I was sittin' there naked as a jaybird
having bet my boots and ultrasuede jacket
and Fiorucci jeans and cheap workshirt
all full of dirt,
and Simple says I ain't got equity
and could ya cash a check, I ask,
and Big Dick puts up his refrigerator
and stove and dishwasher,
and I let him hold my blank check,
and it was almost time to declare our hands.

OH MAN, IT WAS SO DAMN BAD
WE BET EVERYTHING WE HAD
AND BIG DICK CALLED "TIME" AND IT
WAS ME, BAD AL, WHO SAID "HAH,
TIME IS ALL I GOT LEFT.

So we all stick something in our hand
in order to declare,
one if you're goin' high,
none if you're goin' low,
two if you're goin' both ways
and then everybody pays.

OH NO, SIMPLE SIMON'S GOIN' LOW.
OH NO, ROTGUT'S GOT NO CHIP TO SHOW.
OH NO, DOC'S OPENING UP AN EMPTY HAND.
OH NO, BIG DICK'S CHIP HAS TURNED TO SAND.
OH NO, BAD AL IS GOIN' LOW.
OH NO, THE BOYS GOT NOTHIN', NOTHIN' TO SHOW.
OH NO, NO ONE'S GOIN' STRAIGHT.
OH NO, NO ONE'S GOT A PAIR.
OH NO, EVERYONE'S GOIN' LOW.
OH NO, HOW LOW CAN YOU GO.
HOW LOW CAN YOU GO?
HOW LOW CAN YOU GO?

MUTHAH HUBBARD

"GRR," SAYS MAH BELLY,
"GRR," SAYS MAH SNEER.
"AIN'T NOTHIN', NO NOTHIN'
NEVER NOTHIN' IN HERE."

"Grr," I says to this skinny fat cat
who's happy as a clam in the sand
back of his South Hampton mansion
jammin' his hand into the antique can
containin' tongue-teasin' steamers
and when yer a dreamer
the world's yer fuckin' oyster.
He's ready to pop
another denizen of the deep
'cause venison's too steep
out of season (even for him)
and "peep" keeps cheepin' from
the kitchen where the cook
checks his recipe book and whack:
chicken's little neck.
The sky is fallin'
and the guests are ballin'
and I guess it's all in the game.

"Shucks," he giggles as one wriggles
out of his butter fingers.
"Grr," I says and I shuck him.
I rip him open from the chin down,
all around, like when
you take the cardboard tube
in the middle of a toilet paper roll
and tear it apart by the spiral seam.
It's the American dream.
Seems he's had his fill:
suckling pigs and orange ducks
and ol' Empty Belly shucks
and finds cream sauces and exotic salads
that he tosses to the masses in the streets
who don't have no eats,
who shoot up on sweets,
who come 'round for these taboo treats
every twenty years or so.
But the good loins
the rich guy bought with his good coins
are all processed into pre-puke
so not even Dirty Duke,
a love-and food-starved radical of the sixties,
can dig into this human can of worms.
It burns yer nose and eyes and tongue.
Ya put yer hand in this can-opened man
and scoop up the free meal yer entitled to
and pee yoo it stinks like the shit
it's turnin' into.

"GRR," SAYS MAH BELLY,
"GRR," SAYS MAH SNEER.
"AIN'T NOTHIN', NO NOTHIN',
NEVER NOTHIN' IN HERE."

"Grr," I says, c'mere Emir
with yer big beer belly
and yer austere pose.
Abdul, I know yer full of oil
'cause I see it sneakin' up
leakin' up outta the pothole pores
in yer snothole nose.
All I need's a hose
to empty ya down to yer toes.
Last winter I fuckin' froze
'cause heatin' oil costs more
than eatin' oil imported from Greece--
how come they don't fleece us?
They got class, Abdul.
And I got a sharp piece of glass, Abdul,
that's goin' upside yer ass, Abdul,
'cause the price of gas is gonna be so high
soon it'll be cheaper
to fly to the moon, and me,
I never could afford
the price of a round-trip ticket.
You're wicked, Abdul.
Which is why I'm gonna stick it
to ya good, ya ghoul;
I'm gonna twist it
till yer blood starts gushin'
and even the Russians
won't want you when I'm through.
Can ya tell I'm mad?
Doncha know I'm bad?

Bad Al, nobody's pal.
I'm puttin' an Exxon the spot
where you're tryin' to clot
and the odds are even if yer odd man out
you can fill 'er up today,
hooray, olé,
and you don't even have to pay.
But when I pump him,
Abdul plays the fool.
"I don't know nothin'," he smiles
and you can't get too many miles
on the fuel tricklin' out of his veins.
I think it's his brains turned into gruel,
melted and mealy, cut with couscous,
lookin' a little like
chunky-style pineapple juicejuice,
rustin' the insides of our tin tanks,
and that's the thanks we get
for tryin' to dilute the loot
in ol' Emir's banks
which is the final solution.
Remember the American Revolution?

"GRR," SAYS MAH CHEVY,
"GRR," SAYS MAH SNEER.
"AIN'T NOTHIN', NO NOTHIN',
NEVER NOTHIN' IN HERE."

"Grr," I says to Mister Officer Sargent
Doctor Senior Vee Pee
lookin' down his upturned nose at me;
his job is to keep me free
--but the things I need ain't,
they cost dough-re-mi,
gimme dough-re-mi,
gimme everything I see: wheee!
He's got more money
than anyone ever saw
at one time in one pocket,
he better lock it up,
he better hide the key,
he better keep his eye on me
'cause I'm comin' for it,
I'm hummin' and strummin' for it,
I'm gunnin' for his dough-re-mi,
gimme dough-re-mi,
gimme everything I see.
I'm gonna take it
and if Mister Officer Sargent
Doctor Senior Vee Pee
raises his hand I'm gonna break it,
'cause when it comes to money
I just can't make it,
my ends don't meet, defeat,
all potatoes and no meat,
layin' in bed in the heat
or the sleet or on a slab of concrete
--it's all the same sheet.
But Mister's got blisters
countin' all that glisters
from smart tax deals,
and Gee Officer Krupke
peels a fifty off his nifty pay hike
and him and Pottsy and Pat and Mike
would like to toast all the young cops

on their big bad bikes
who'll be the first to go
when there ain't no more dough;
and Sarge has a large GI stipend
till the end of his days
and everybody pays the Doc
until they're in hock
and Senior Vee Pee's got a lock
on six-digit salaries
while I'm workin' with a wage freeze.
But I ain't gettin' down on my knees.
I ain't sayin' please.
I'm walkin' right up to yer vault,
mah wounds full of yer salt,
and I'm gonna light the fuse,
I'm gonna collect my dues,
I got nothin' to lose.
Boom. But uh oh. Gloom.
Yer stuff's still safe
even though I blew yer safe away.
There ain't no cash: Smash.
There ain't no gelt: Belt.
There ain't no jack: Whack.
Only plastic, only checkbooks,
only stock certificates,
only insurance policies,
only pension plans,
only deeds and liens and loans,
only funds and bonds and no bones.
No bones.
Not a single bone for this poor ol' dog.

"GRR," SAYS MAH BELLY,
"GRR," SAYS MAH SNEER.
"AIN'T NOTHIN', NO NOTHIN'
NEVER NOTHIN' IN HERE."

It stinks. It stinks and it stinks and it stinks
and it stinks.

                    --C.K. Williams